The difference between an A student and a C student is EXPOSURE and WORK ETHIC.

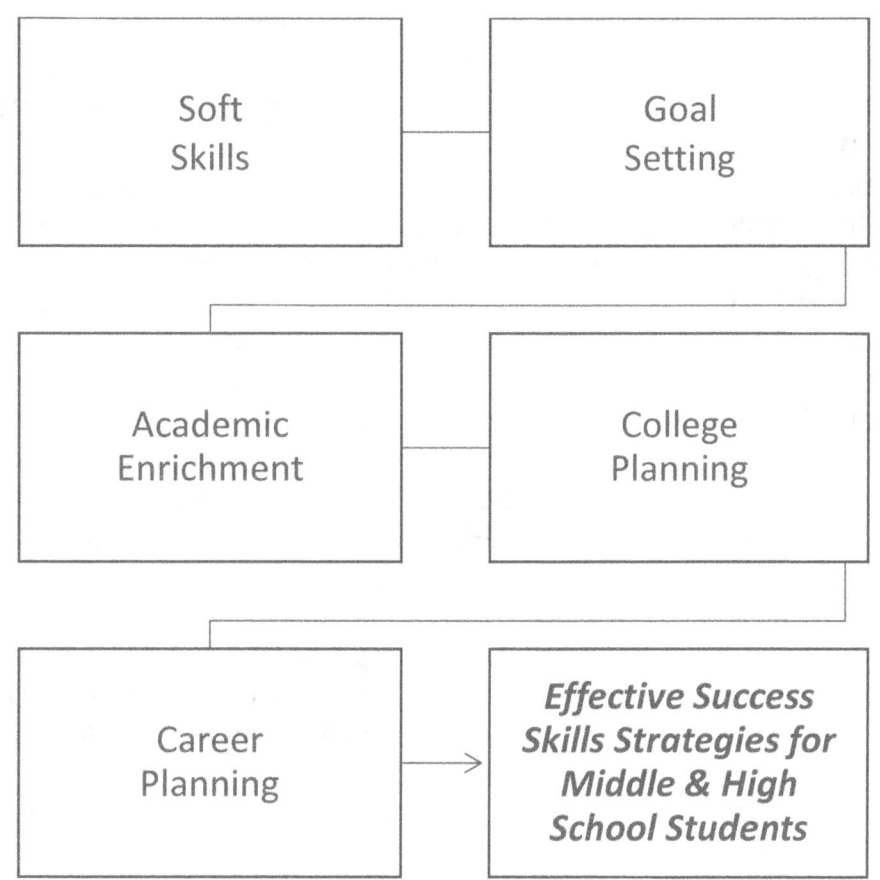

Kimberly W. Daniel, M.Ed., GCDF
Keystone Instructional Services, Inc.
Atlanta, GA

Copyright © 2017 by Kimberly Wilson Daniel
All Rights reserved.
Printed in the United States of America
ISBN – 9780692869543

www. keystoneinstructionalservices.com

Dear Student:

I have had the opportunity to learn and implement the success strategies you are about to be exposed to through the Start Right..Stay Right program. Through this program, I learned to try new things. You'll never know what you like or want in life until you try new things. Think about it, if you wake up every morning and perform the same routine, your life will never have anything new to offer. How will you know what your favorite ice cream flavor is if you haven't tried new ones? If you never try new things, you may never know what other opportunities may come out of them.

You must remember that opportunities are created, not given and it's important to take advantage of them because they work in somewhat of a slippery slope logical fallacy where one thing leads to another. For example, Ms. Daniel had a guest speaker come in and talk about a program that focused on entrepreneurial skill enhancement. I decided to consider the program and eventually applied. Going into the program with no idea of how things worked, I was able to build relationships to the point where I was elected President. In the program, not only was I gaining knowledge on small business startup, but I was able to network with a multitude of people ranging from the CEO of Chick-Fil-A to the top accountants that work at UPS. Fortunately, our student company performance allowed us to be the top company in Georgia and we will proceed to the national competition in Washington, D.C. Think about this though, if I would have never taken advantage of this opportunity, I would not have been able to network with such high-level people, gain entrepreneurship skills, or even have plans of going to Washington for nationals. When you open one door, it leads to another.

Another success strategy that I've learned through Ms. Daniel's program is to stand out in a positive way as much as possible. You shouldn't be the leader of the pack all the time. Of course, you want to be a leader but you also need to be surrounded by people who possess qualities that will help you grow. Surround yourself with people who will help you excel. This means networking with people who know what you don't so that they can teach you.

I want to thank Ms. Daniel because with the success strategies that I've been given, my chances of excelling in my career of choice have increased tremendously. Without these strategies, I would be far short the amount of experiences and interpersonal skills that I possess today. This program is responsible for many of the things I've been able to partake in as well as the new knowledges I have in small business startup and entrepreneurship.

Enjoy the journey,

Jaylin Grier
NSCHS, 11th Grade Student

A Message from the Author...

Dear student:

I am so excited to have you join forces with the other students who have participated in the Start Right..Stay Right program. The goal of the program is to make sure you get on the right path to the future you want for yourself. My students often call me the "Quote Lady." I enjoy finding quotes that inspire me. I found all the quotes that I put in this manual on BrainyQuote.com. I hope they inspire you to strive for greatness in all that you do.

Every year that I teach the program, I am overwhelmed by the transformation that I see take place in the lives of my students from the beginning of the program and through each year of their lives. I didn't say until the end of the program because the skills and tools they develop continue to work as they progress through life.

This student program manual consists of strategies & skills organized under five modules. Each module contains a series of lessons that will introduce you to tools and strategies you can use to establish and incorporate effective habits that will move you forward as a successful individual who is prepared to not only excel in school but also in life.

My desire is to provide opportunities which introduce, develop, and reinforce the academic and occupational knowledge, skills, and attitudes you will need to graduate from high school and transition effectively into technical school, college, the armed forces, or the workforce. Working with students assisting them in determining their personal goals, core values, and college and career goals is one of the highlights of my career.

The lessons and activities in the manual will give you the skills and knowledge you need to stay focused throughout the years as you move forward on your journey to the college and career of your dreams!

Enjoy the journey!

Kimberly W. Daniel, M.Ed., GCDF
Director, Keystone Instructional Services, Inc.

"We are what we repeatedly do. Excellence then is not an act, but a habit." **Aristotle**

How to Utilize the Start Right..Stay Right Program

Each lesson gives you an opportunity to explore real world lessons that will teach you skills you can implement immediately into your daily routine.

Read through the lessons and really connect with what is being taught. At the end of each lesson, you will either complete a reflection where you will reflect upon what you learned and plan a strategy for implementation of the new skills into your own daily routine or complete an activity that reinforces the skills you learned.

If you commit wholeheartedly to implementing the strategies outlined in this program, upon completion, you will have an excellent resource that will assist you as you navigate through school and as you transition to your chosen college and/or career.

TABLE OF CONTENTS

Module 1: Soft Skills
- Integrity 6
- Conflict Resolution 7
- Communication Skills 8
- Critical Thinking 9
- Decision Making 10
- Teamwork 12
- Work Ethic 13
- Time Management 14

Module 2: Academic Enrichment
- Reading Strategies 16
- Note-taking Strategies 18
- Study Skills 20
- Test Taking Strategies 22
- Tutoring/Afterschool Academic Enrichment/Online Resources 24

Module 3: Goal Setting
- Setting Goals 26
- Intrinsic Motivation 28
- Academic/Extracurricular Goal Setting 30
- Setting an Academic Goal 31
- Setting an Extracurricular Goal 32

Module 4: College Planning
- Interest Survey 33
- Career Choices 35
- Colleges - Technical vs. Community College vs. University 36
- How to Find Out More About a College 37
- College Costs/Financial Aid/Scholarships 39
- Finding Scholarships 41
- ACT/SAT 42

Module 5: Career Planning
- Choosing the Right Career 43

Culminating Assessment: Vision Board Project 45

Final Reflection 47

Closing Thoughts 48

Glossary 49

Module 1: Soft Skills

Integrity

"Integrity gives you real freedom because you have nothing to fear since you have nothing to hide." **Zig Ziglar**

What is integrity and why is so important?

According to the Cambridge Dictionary, **integrity** is "the quality of being honest and having strong moral principles." When someone uses the phrase "a person of integrity" to describe you, they believe you are a person who is honest and fair. They don't believe you are a perfect person, but they feel when you are faced with difficult decisions, you will make honest impartial choices that will benefit the good of the whole, not just yourself.

It takes courage to exhibit integrity. Sometimes you will be judged unfairly for standing up for what you believe is right. Not everyone will stand up for someone who is being bullied or make an extra effort to sit with someone who is all alone.

Integrity is a character trait that is developed as you get older. Its development is fostered by the morals and values that your parents or other adults instill in you. Have you ever been in a situation where a store clerk gave you too much change? What did you do? Did you leave out of the store without saying anything or did you tell the clerk about the mistake?

People of integrity can be trusted to do the right thing even in difficult or tempting situations and as time passes, these people often become role models. They are not seeking this title; it comes naturally because of their commitment to doing the right thing regardless of the circumstance.

Reflection:
Think of someone you consider to be a role model. List 5 characteristics this person possesses that makes them a role model.
1.
2.
3.
4.
5.

Implementation:
Of the 5 characteristics you listed, which ones do you already possess and which do you need to improve upon?

_____
_____
_____
_____

Module 1: Soft Skills

Conflict Resolution

"Peace is not absence of conflict; it is the ability to handle conflict by peaceful means." **Ronald Reagan**

Being able to work through conflict effectively encompasses the utilization of many character traits to actually pull it off. You must be able to listen objectively, exercise patience, and be willing to put personal feelings aside. There will be situations where conflict cannot be avoided. It is a part of life. We live in a world where people don't always agree. Despite your personal feelings, you will have to do what is best for your family, your school, your team, the company you work for, or even your own business. It is during these times when you must keep a cool head and always think about the consequences of your actions.

Have you ever been to a restaurant and witnessed a patron being disrespectful to a server? Did that server remain professional even though the patron was irate or did the server react poorly in the situation? A person who is able to effectively deal with conflict will always be able to see beyond the current situation and understand their reaction to the circumstances is more important than the person's actions.

Athletes who exhibit good sportsmanship understand the principles of conflict resolution. There are many times when an athlete is put in a situation where they must exercise a great deal of self-discipline and they do not allow their emotions to dictate their behavior. You never know who is watching your reaction and if you react poorly, it could cost the team the game or even result in loss of scholarship opportunities.

Reflection:
Take a moment and think about a time when you had a conversation with someone about a touchy subject and the conversation turned into an argument. How could the situation have turned out differently?

_____
_____
_____

Implementation:
If you worked in customer service and a customer was being rude and extremely loud, how would you handle the situation?

_____
_____
_____
_____

Module 1: Soft Skills

Communication Skills

"Intelligence, knowledge or experience are important and might get you a job, but strong communication skills are what will get you promoted." **Mireille Giliano**

Many people consider communication to be simply talking to someone. However, the most important part of effective communication is listening. When we listen effectively, we are more apt to not only hear what the person is saying but also listen to their tone, pay attention to their body language, and the delivery of the message. What people see when you are speaking to them is just as important as what they hear.

Have you ever had a conversation with your parents and even though you were listening, you were also busy doing something else and you hear them ask, "Are you listening to me?" They're asking because they are not receiving your undivided attention. They can tell that what they are saying is going in one ear and out the other. Their message is not being received.

You must spend time practicing effective listening and speaking so you can develop effective communication skills. Technology is wonderful however it has lessened the need for actual verbal communication. It is much more convenient to text or email what needs to be said. However, what will happen when you are in a scholarship or job interview and you must communicate with people on the interview panel? You may be the perfect candidate but if you don't possess effective communication skills, you will not be perceived as someone who is knowledgeable. What happens when you are in an important company meeting and it is your turn to present a proposal for a new multi-million-dollar project? Will you be able to deliver the proposal in a manner that persuades those in attendance to accept what you are proposing?

In order to practice your communication skills, you must spend time communicating. Group projects, oral presentations, and simple conversations in the cafeteria or at the dinner table are all opportunities for effective communication.

Reflection:
How much time do you spend communicating without technology each day?

0 – 1 hour   1 – 2 hours   2 -3 hours   3 – 4 hours   More than 4 hours

Implementation:
Think about a time when you were listening to respond instead of truly listening to the person. What can you do to prevent these types of situations?

_____
_____
_____
_____

Module 1: Soft Skills

Critical Thinking

"Coming up with a way to fix mistakes challenges your creativity and your critical thinking skills and your resourcefulness. Often you end up with something better than what you planned on in the first place." **Mark Frauenfelder**

Effective critical thinking skills are needed to solve problems. There will be times when you are faced with a situation where you have been given various types of information and asked to draw your own conclusions. Many times, the information you have will be just the basics. You must learn to put on your detective hat and begin to question how it all ties together and predict what will happen when you manipulate the information. How you process and manipulate the information will determine if you are able to develop an effective conclusion or solution. The phrase," Because I said so," tends to work only with parents. Often when there is valid reasoning behind your thoughts, people are more apt to deem you as credible whether they agree or not.

Who likes math word problems? When you read the problem, it always seems as though valuable information was left out. Even though it seems impossible to solve in the beginning, once you begin to analyze the information you are given, you begin to understand how the information correlates and can be used to solve the problem. Working through math problems may seem tedious and unnecessary now but you are gaining valuable skills that will help you solve the problems you will encounter later on in life. Critical thinking is often a process that takes place during half-time of any sporting event. The coach has to decide how to help the team keep the lead or take the lead.

People with critical thinking skills are able to determine correlations between ideas and processes then use what they discover to make predictions and inferences. They are able to approach problems and issues with a strategic method that will enable them to move towards the solution. They also have ample experience working through difficult situations and they are less likely to "crack under pressure."

Reflection:
Describe a time when things were not going well for you and you had to sit down and create a plan to change things for the better.

_____
_____
_____

Implementation:
List steps you can take to exercise your brain muscle by thinking critically?

_____
_____
_____

Module 1: Soft Skills

Decision Making

"Inability to make decisions is one of the principal reasons executives fail. Deficiency in decision-making ranks much higher than lack of specific knowledge or technical know-how as an indicator of leadership failure."
John C. Maxwell

With every decision comes a consequence therefore, you must do your best to weigh out the cost before making a decision. There will be times when you are not able to sit and analyze the circumstances before making a decision and during those times, you will have to rely on good judgement and hope for the best. However, in most cases, there is ample time to survey the situation and determine the best choice to make.

You will make lots of decisions every day. Some are menial as toast or biscuit, orange or apple. However, others can have more serious consequences such as whether or not you should cut class or cheat on a test. Whenever you are faced with the task of making a big decision, you should always "play the tape to the end." In other words, think the decision all the way through. For example, should you cut class? It really seems like a relatively easy decision to make. One time is not such a big deal, right? Wrong. There is so much more to consider. What about the instruction you miss? What happens if you get caught? What will your parents say? There are a ton of consequences to consider before going forward with the decision to cut class. Make sure you consider the pros and the cons of the decision because decisions made now can have a devastating effect on your future.

What about the decision to buy a new car? It's the newest model and it's a gorgeous car. The offer says no down payment. It seems like a great idea at first but what about the car payment that will be due every month for the next four to five years? What about the insurance payment, the gas prices, the maintenance costs? When considering some of the factors, some people decide that the car they currently have is really not that bad at all.

You will not make the best decision every time. Sometimes you gain valuable experience from bad decisions and failures. Try to avoid making a poor decision but if you make one, be sure to learn the lesson because then, you should be able to avoid making the poor decision again. That shows growth and maturity.

Reflection:
Describe a situation where you made a poor decision and a situation where you made a good decision, what were the consequences of both?

_____
_____
_____
_____

Implementation:
List three things you should do before making a decision?

_____
_____
_____
_____

Module 1: Soft Skills

Teamwork

"Individual commitment to a group effort--that is what makes a team work, a company work, a society work, a civilization work." **Vince Lombardi**

Being able to work well with others is an essential component to teamwork. Think about a time in school when the teacher announced the requirements for a group project and you would not be able to choose your own partners. Cue the rolled eyes and loud sighs. No one wants to be placed in a group with a person who does not know how to work well with others or with the person who is always a slacker. There is always the fear of a bad grade because someone in the group is not willing to do their part or what's best for the group.

The purpose of teamwork is to be able to divide and conquer. Each person knows their tasks and they work to the best of their ability towards completing those tasks. If they run into difficulties, they know they can rely on their teammates for assistance. Being a successful unit is of the utmost importance. "All for one and one for all" is the mantra of a great team.

When given a task, a great team will begin by discovering each other's strengths and assigning roles based on those strengths. Your team is more likely to succeed when individuals are operating in their strengths. For example, if your strength is drawing, maybe you should ask to be in charge of all of the illustrations or visuals for the project. Another person whose strength is speaking may choose to deliver the message. Dividing the work provides opportunities for getting a great deal of work done in a short period of time.

The teamwork skills you learn while working on group projects, playing a sport, or serving in a leadership role for an extra-curricular club will transfer wherever you go in life. These skills will prove beneficial in the years to come because you will be faced with many opportunities that will require you to work as part of a team. Based on your experiences, you will be able to communicate effectively, make valid contributions to the group, and utilize good decision-making skills.

Reflection:
When working with a team, what are your strengths and weaknesses?
_____
_____
_____

Implementation:
What steps can you take to be a more effective member of a team?
_____
_____
_____

Module 1: Soft Skills

Work Ethic

"I've been blessed with a lot of great things in my life, and one of them was work ethic. And with work ethic, you can make anything happen." **Jon Runyan**

According to the Cambridge Dictionary, **work ethic** is "the belief that work is valuable as an activity and is morally good." In order to achieve the goals you have set for yourself, you must possess a strong work ethic. People with strong work ethic understand they must persevere through procrastination and distractions and commit to completing the task at hand to the best of their ability. People with strong work ethic assume responsibility for their outcomes in life. They take pride in their performance and understand that if they succeed or fail it is because of their commitment or lack thereof to their goals.

When teachers or leaders speak of students with strong work ethic, they often use terms such as disciplined, hard worker, committed, and dependable. Think about that student who always turns their work in on time, is never late for class, and is always prepared. That is a student with strong work ethic. Perhaps they have set a goal to get an A in the class or maybe this is a student who has failed a class before and has made the decision not to fail again. In either case, there is a commitment to staying focused and working hard.

Many people with poor work ethic tend to have regrets later in life. On graduation day, there will be students who will not walk across the stage and receive their diploma, not because they weren't smart enough but because they lacked work ethic. Some students who graduate will simply wear a cap and gown while others will be decorated with cords and stoles that signify their participation in extracurricular activities and excellence in the classroom. Other students will struggle to find ways to pay for college because they were turned down for scholarships due to poor grades and lack of community service. They assumed they had all the time in the world to take care of those things so there was no rush. Then there will be those students who will have many opportunities because of their strong work ethic. They will be accepted into many colleges and awarded many scholarships to help pay their tuition. Which will you be?

Reflection:
List the character traits of someone you know who has strong work ethic.
_____
_____
_____

Implementation:
What steps could you take to ensure you make it to class on time each day?
_____
_____
_____

Module 1: Soft Skills

Time Management

"He, who every morning plans the transactions of the day, and follows that plan, carries a thread that will guide him through a labyrinth of the most busy life."
Victor Hugo

What are you doing with most of your time each day? Students are involved in many activities inside and outside of school. Due to such an active schedule, time management is imperative. For some students, their biggest timewasters are spending hours watching TV/Movies, surfing the internet, posting on social media, or playing video games. The first step to managing your time wisely is figuring out what you are currently spending your time doing and then developing a plan that includes some of your time wasters but more of the important things like homework, studying, community service, family time, etc.

Often times, we tend to put the things we want to do ahead of the things we need to do and we end up not having enough time to complete the most important tasks of the day. When you make your to do list, be sure to incorporate the tasks you have to accomplish as well as some of the fun things you enjoy doing each day. This will help ensure your day is not all work and it will help solve the "I didn't have enough time" problem.

Have you ever started playing a game on your phone and before you knew it, a couple of hours had passed? That's literally what the phrase, "Time flies when you're having fun" means. You are so engrossed in the activity that you don't even realize that hours have passed by. Then you start the mad rush to get your homework done or study for a test but before you can even get started good, here comes the yawn. You're just too tired so you decide you will go to sleep and get up earlier the next morning. However, the next morning comes and you're rushing because you overslept, you forgot to get your clothes out, you have to pack your book bag and make it to the bus stop in time.

Taking the time to prioritize your day takes discipline and commitment. However, if you are able to master the art of effective time management, you will discover there is more than enough time to accomplish your daily goals and spend time doing some of the things you enjoy.

Reflection:

Time management skills are very important. Habits are formed when a person does something repeatedly. It becomes second nature. What habits do you have that impact your time management skills in a positive way and in a negative way?

_____
_____
_____
_____

Implementation:

What can you do to change those negative habits into positive habits?

_____
_____
_____
_____

Module 2: Academic Enrichment

Reading Strategies

"Reading is to the mind what exercise is to the body." **Joseph Addison**

Annotate..Annotate..Annotate...That is the word for today! If you haven't already been taught how to annotate, LEARN! This will help you with your reading comprehension and retention. If you're like many readers, you can read the same passage three times and forget what the beginning was about before you get to the middle each time. Nothing seems to work. You read, re-read, and re-read again and you still have trouble drawing conclusions or remembering what you read. Many students still live with that image of the Media Specialist standing over them saying, "DO NOT WRITE IN THE BOOKS!" and that's is a perfectly valid statement. The books belong to the Media Center and must be kept in good shape. But, for your own personal books, handouts, notes, or whatever...ANNOTATE. Annotating helps you stay focused. You are less likely to "zone out" if you are actively processing information while you are reading.

Marking the text and annotating will help you better comprehend the material you are reading. As you read, underline the main ideas and highlight pertinent information. Be sure to jot down any thoughts or questions that come to mind. These can be thoughts that help you relate to the text. Each time you relate what you are reading to something that happened to you personally, or to a friend, or even to something you saw on television, you are processing the information in a meaningful way and you are more likely to remember that information due to the relationship you made. When the teacher discusses the text, add to your annotations. If a peer adds something of value to the discussion, make sure you write that in your margins as well. If you wrote down a question about the text during the group discussion, ask a peer or the teacher for clarification then make a note of the additional information you gained.

Another strategy to help with comprehension is to circle any terms you do not know. Take the time to look up the definitions so you will understand how they are being used in the text. Write the meaning in the margins. If you understand the vocabulary that is being used, you will begin to understand the text more. When you go back to review or study for a test, your review time is more meaningful because you have supporting information to help you comprehend the material better.

Reflection:
On a scale of 1 to 10 (1 lowest – 10 highest), how well would you rate your reading skills?

        1   2   3   4   5   6   7   8   9   10

Implementation:
What strategies can you implement each day to improve your reading skills?

_____
_____
_____

Module 2: Academic Enrichment

Note-taking Strategies

"Whatever the difference between brilliant and average brains, we are all creative. And through practice and study we can enhance our skills and talents. **Jeff Hawkins**

There are various methods for taking notes. As a learner, you must find the note-taking strategies that will best help you retain the information you are learning. Whether you are taking notes from a lecture, video, or PowerPoint, the key strategies are the same – know what to write down, understand the purpose of reviewing and revising your notes often, and use your notes to quiz yourself as you prepare for the test.

Have you ever been in class with that student who tries to write down every word the teacher says? They are often asking the teacher to repeat a statement or asking them to return to the previous slide so they could write down everything. This is not effective note-taking. Valuable information like questions from your peers and extended information that the teacher is sharing to make the lesson more relevant is missed during this method. As a note taker, you have to become a detective. You have to learn how to determine what information is filer and what information is pertinent. I know you're probably thinking, "why can't the teacher just tell me what will be on the test and then I will write that down." Well, if you are continuously spoon fed information in this manner, you will never develop the critical thinking skills you will need in college and the workforce. Some of your best lessons will be learned from your most challenging assignments.

Some note-taking strategies that will help you retain information include listening attentively, writing down only the pertinent information, writing legible short phrases and not sentences, leaving blank space so that you can go back and annotate your notes, re-writing your notes, comparing your notes with your peers to be sure you have the necessary information, using your notes to develop questions you think the teacher may ask, and most important, going over your notes multiple times using meaningful retention strategies that will help you retain the information. Cramming is never the best choice. Setting aside time that is devoted strictly to studying your notes each night will prove more beneficial in the long run.

Reflection:
On a scale of 1 to 10 (1 lowest – 10 highest), how well would you rate your note-taking skills?

        1   2   3   4   5   6   7   8   9   10

Implementation:
What strategies can you implement to improve your note-taking skills?

_____
_____
_____
_____

Module 2: Academic Enrichment

Study Skills

"The roots of education are bitter, but the fruit is sweet." **Aristotle**

Let's be honest, most people do not like to study. Some feel it's a waste of time. They spend hours reading over their notes and then discover what they spent most of their time studying wasn't even on the test. Others get home and start to study and they don't know where to begin. They have notes but they don't seem to make sense now that the teacher is not around. Some even believe cramming is better than studying until they ace the quiz but somehow fail the unit test.

Have you really stopped and took the time to examine your study habits? How often do you study? Where do you study? Do you listen to music, have your phone out, or have the TV on while you study? How long do you study? The answers to these questions should be considered when determining if your study methods are effective. Today, more than ever, we live in a world full of distractions. Many people feel they are able to do many things while studying but in actuality, they should be devoting all of their efforts during their study time to doing just that – studying. But, let's face it, many people do not know how to study effectively.

There are ways to make your study time more productive. You should try many techniques until you find the ones that best fit your learning style. Be sure to find a quiet place to designate as your study area. Make sure your area is equipped with all of the materials you need but more importantly, it should be designated as your "distraction free" zone. There should be no television, radio, cell phone or tablet (unless you need to do research), video games, etc. It might seem harsh at first but this area should be the place you go to concentrate solely on your studies. Remember that lesson on time management. When you set up your priority list, you designated time for studying and you allotted time for the other things you enjoy doing as well.

Changing your study habits will take discipline and commitment. It will seem tedious and burdensome in the beginning as do most things that we must learn for the first time but your hard work will pay off. Set a timer for 30 minutes. Study for those 30 minutes with no distractions then give yourself a 10-minute break. Repeat this until your task is complete. Making a commitment to come home and devote 2 hours of your afternoon to homework and studying each day could mean the difference between you failing a course or passing with a B. All the grades you receive for high school courses are used to calculate your Grade Point Average (GPA). This is a calculation that will be used to determine whether you are accepted to college or awarded scholarships. Obtaining the highest GPA possible will only benefit you in the future. However, the long-term benefits will more than just a great GPA. It will also be the establishment of study habits that work and a realization that studying is actually cool.

Reflection:
On a scale of 1 to 10 (1 lowest – 10 highest), how well would you rate your study skills?

        1   2   3   4   5   6   7   8   9   10

Implementation:
What strategies can you implement each day to improve your study skills?
_____
_____
_____
_____

Module 2: Academic Enrichment

Test Taking Strategies

"There are no secrets to success. It is the result of preparation, hard work, and learning from failure." **Colin Powell**

Are you that student who is super nervous because today It is test day? You've studied and you're ready but you are still a nervous wreck. Tests are given to measure your level of understanding of the material. While they are not perfect measures, they give the teacher an understanding of what you've learned and what needs to be retaught. There are many strategies that will help you improve your test taking abilities. If you are following the strategies you outlined for yourself in the time management and study strategies lessons, cramming should not be necessary. You should only need to complete a review session the night before the test. Remember, nothing beats proper preparation.

Prior to the test, make sure you get a proper night's rest, drink plenty of water, and eat a balanced breakfast/lunch on test day. Being fully hydrated and properly nourished will help you stay focused and alert. When it is time to take the test make sure you write your name on the test. I know that seems crazy, huh? But, that is a very common mistake. Next, read the directions carefully. You want to make sure you fully understand what you are supposed to be doing before you start. Getting half-way through the test and realizing you've been doing portions of it wrong could prove disastrous. Then, quickly scan through the test to see what you are expected to complete in the time frame allotted for taking the test.

When you read a question, pay attention to the details. This will help you focus on the pertinent information. After reading the question, read all of the choices before making your decision. Try to eliminate the choices that are obviously wrong and then select the best answer. Proceed one question at a time but don't spend too much time on one question. If the question seems too difficult, skip it and come back to it later. The answer may be found in another question later in the test so again, be sure to read every question.

If you have been preparing for this test and utilizing effective study strategies and you come across a puzzling question, go with your instinct, trust your first thought. And what about those discussion questions? Some people miss the biggest opportunity to gain points by simply answering with a few words. This is your time to demonstrate what you've learned. When answering discussion questions, be sure to answer every part of the question. Don't be in a rush just to write something down. Organize your thoughts and put together a well thought out answer that covers everything the question asks. By doing so, you are more likely to get the maximum amount of points for your answer.

After you have answered all the questions you feel comfortable with, go back and make an educated guess at the ones you skipped. Then before you submit your test, look back over it to make sure you have not left any questions unanswered. Once it is safe to take out your notes, go through and highlight, circle, or underline the information that was on the test. This will help you prepare for the major assessment or final exam. Remember to stay positive always.

Reflection:
On a scale of 1 to 10 (1 lowest – 10 highest), how well would you rate your test taking skills?

        1   2   3   4   5   6   7   8   9   10

Implementation:
What strategies can you implement each day to improve your test taking skills?

_____
_____
_____
_____

Module 2: Academic Enrichment

Tutoring/Afterschool Academic Enrichment/Online Resources

"I loved getting tutored and having that one-on-one attention that you sometimes do not get in regular school." **Tia Mowry**

Many resources are available to enhance your level of learning. Tutoring gives you the opportunity to have a more focused learning session with a teacher. You can concentrate on the areas where you are experiencing confusion or you can simply go to reinforce what you learned in class that day. At the beginning of each course, you should find out what days your teacher will offer tutoring opportunities. These times may be before or after school. Adjust your schedule to be able to attend at least two tutoring sessions per week.

If your school does not offer tutoring, many online services are available that can enrich your learning. When searching for online resources, you can use search engines to find video tutorials, extra homework practice, and extension activities that will help you understand the material more. With the advancement in technology, it is even possible to video chat with teachers who can provide assistance. Many textbook companies provide an online platform where students can log in and find extra instruction via presentations and sample tests. Mastering activities beyond the classroom will help you prepare for unit tests and major assessments.

Develop Your Academic Enrichment Plan

Complete the table by finding out what day and time your teacher will offer tutoring opportunities AND list at least 1 extra activity you will do on your own for each subject.
(And yes, sometimes teachers do study sessions on the weekends.)

Course Name	Mon.	Tues.	Weds.	Thurs.	Fri.	Sat.	Sun.

Course Name	Mon.	Tues.	Weds.	Thurs.	Fri.	Sat.	Sun.

Module 3: Goal Setting

Setting Goals

"A goal without a plan is just a wish." **Jeff Rich**

Why is goal setting important? Proceeding through life without setting goals will leave you without a map to guide you along your journey to success. It's like deciding to drive across the country without a map. You have not planned out the trip. It might take you much longer than you expected or you may never make it. When we write out our goals and post them, we are more likely to remember them and work towards accomplishing them. It is also important to share your goals with people who will hold you accountable. For example, if you set a short term goal of having a B in math at the end of every 9 weeks and you communicate this goal with a parent, they will be able to hold you accountable by making sure you are studying, reminding you of your goal if you bring home a grade below a B, and congratulating you along the way for working hard to accomplish the goal you have set for yourself.

Effective goal setting focuses on short and long range goals. Goal setting can be as simple as planning to save $50 by the end of the school year to as complex as becoming an Astronaut by the age of 35. Both goals still have to be divided into a series of steps and then accomplishment of each step puts you one step closer to accomplishing the goal. Often times, when you break down your long term goals into a series of short term goals, you don't get bogged down and discouraged by all of the tasks needed to accomplish the main goal. Checking off each goal and rewarding yourself along the way gives you a sense of accomplishment and helps you stay focused on making it to the finish line.

The main points to remember when making goals are to make sure they are important enough to inspire you to persevere through obstacles and overcome distractions. When you sit down and begin crafting your goals, think about where you would like to see yourself in 10 years. What is your family structure like? Are you married or single? Do you live in a house or an apartment? Do you live in a big city or a rural area? Do you work in an office or lab? Design your future. Once you have done this, develop a plan to make it happen. What will it take to live according to your desires? Do you need a college degree? Do you need a special license for this career? There are many things to consider that is why a great deal of thought must go into the goals you set for yourself.

Reflection:
Have you ever made a New Year's resolution that you never accomplished? Discuss the difference between the trend to set a New Year's resolution and true goal setting.

_____
_____
_____
_____

Implementation:
List 1 academic goal that you will commit to working towards during this term.

_____
_____
_____
_____

Module 3: Goal Setting

Intrinsic Motivation

"Good, better, best. Never let it rest. 'Til your good is better and your better is best." **St. Jerome**

When you decide on your goals, there has to be something inside of you that believes so deeply in those goals that nothing and no one can stop you from working to achieve them. That something is called intrinsic motivation. You are not working for fame or fortune or the accolades given by those on the outside. You have a deep-rooted desire to be everything you set out to become. For example, there are people who desire to become doctors not because of the salary that is attached to the career or the nice things that doctors seem to have. Their desire to become a doctor is based upon their desire to help people live healthy lives. They want to make a difference in the well-being of others. The desire is strong and it helps them look beyond the extra years and high cost of medical school to see the ultimate reward they will receive from saving someone's life.

People who are intrinsically motivated do not give up easily. They understand the goals they have set for themselves may be lofty and take time to achieve; nevertheless, they remain committed. When distractions arise that could make them veer off course, they are more apt to recognize the distraction and decide accomplishment of their goals is more important to them. Their level of self-discipline helps them forego watching that marathon of their favorite television show with the understanding that they can record and watch it later.

You are more apt to be intrinsically motivated to accomplish a goal when it is something you choose. That's why you should spend time really developing goals that are meaningful to you. To move from being an extrinsically motivated person where sometimes we are rewarded for doing what we are supposed to do anyway to an intrinsically motivated person, you must have a mind shift. You may be accustomed to receiving a reward for good grades and completing your chores but what happens when there is no external reward to receive? How do you dig deep and do your best when there is nothing to receive but personal satisfaction? When no one is there to pat you on your back and say, "good job," are you able to pat yourself on the back?

Reflection:
Was there a time when you were given a reward for doing what you were truly supposed to be doing anyway? What happened when the reward was no longer available?

_____
_____
_____

Implementation:
Why do you really want to accomplish the goal you committed to in the previous section?

_____
_____
_____

Module 3: Goal Setting

Academic and Extra-Curricular Goal Setting

"Education is the key to unlock the golden door of freedom."
George Washington Carver

Setting goals that are related to your academic career can help drive you to accomplish more than you ever imagined. Simply setting a goal to always be on time to class will help you become a person who values punctuality. This will prove very valuable when you enter the workforce. At the beginning of every school year, you should make your short term goals and reevaluate your progress towards accomplishing your long range goals. It is not enough to simply say you want to be an honor student or you want to get an A in math. You have to create a plan of action that breaks down the actions you will need to take to accomplish the goals.

Opportunities will arise from obtaining good grades in school; however, some students forget how important extracurricular activities are as well. Extracurricular activities may include sports, clubs, academic competitive teams, art and music programs, and community involvement. These types of activities help you develop your talents and passions. They give you valuable experiences that will help you become a well-rounded person. Many scholarship, college, and job applications have a section for you to list the activities outside of the normal required curriculum that you have participated in while in school. Without these activities, you may find that good grades were simply not enough to gain the advantage over other applicants who were involved in many activities.

GOAL SETTING ACTVITIES

On the next two pages, spend time crafting one academic goal and one extracurricular goal for this term. This activity should serve as practice for making goals throughout life. Be sure to make short and long term goals throughout school. Accomplishment of your goals will make you more marketable when applying for scholarships, colleges, and jobs. Re-visit your goals throughout the term to make sure you are on track to accomplishing them. Be sure to share your goals with an adult so they can keep you accountable.

Activity 1 – Create an **<u>academic goal</u>** such as "maintain a B in math class every grading period this term" or "attend tutoring two times per week and turn in all homework assignments on time." Make sure your goal is something you are capable of doing and is something you are passionate about accomplishing. Be sure to revisit this page throughout the term to measure your progress.

This Term - <u>Academic</u>

Why is this goal important to me?

<u>OUTLINE YOUR PATH TO ACCOMPLISHING THIS GOAL</u>

What are 3 action steps I will take to begin working on this goal? (tutoring-when, test corrections-when, turn assignments-when, communicate w/ teacher–when, etc.)

How can I measure my progress? (check online portal-how often, what criteria will you use to determine whether you have met your goal?)

Who will be my support system and when will I discuss my goals with them? (Be specific)

Activity 2 – Create an **extracurricular goal** such as "join FBLA and compete in at least two competitions this term" or "average 3 steals and 4 assists per game this season." Make sure your goal is something you are capable of doing and is something you are passionate about accomplishing. Be sure to revisit this page throughout the term to measure your progress.

This Term - Extracurricular

Why is this goal important to me?

OUTLINE YOUR PATH TO ACCOMPLISHING THIS GOAL

What are 3 action steps I will take to begin working on this goal? (Trying out for a team- when, joining a club-which club, running for a leadership position-which one, etc.)

How can I measure my progress? (Pay club dues - when, working out in the off season - how often), etc.)

Who will be my support system and when will I discuss my goals with them? (Be specific)

Module 4: College Planning

Interest Survey

"Choose a job you love and you will never have to work a day in your life."
Confucius

Students choose colleges to attend for a variety of reasons. Maybe it was the college their parents attended or maybe it's because of their favorite sports team. On occasion, you will hear a student say, "because they have my major." Ensuring you choose a college that has the major that supports your career choice is very important. Unfortunately, many students have no clue about what they want to do after college or if they actually need a 4-year degree for their intended career. Some students are driven by the amount of money they can make in a particular career. Although money is important, it should not be the driving force for choosing your career.

One of the best starting points is to take an interest survey. Interest surveys help you pinpoint tasks you enjoy doing. The results are based on how you answer questions related to whether or not you would enjoy performing particular tasks that are associated with various careers. While the results do not dictate what career you will pursue in life, they give you valuable insight that you can use to narrow down the many available career choices. You should take interest surveys at different time periods in your life because the results you receive as an 8th grader may differ from the results you receive as an 11th grader. A great deal can change in three years due to exposure to more careers and opportunities.

Follow the steps in this lesson to get an understanding of what your current interests are and what careers match those interests. Go to **www.Mynextmove.org** to complete the interest survey sponsored by the US Department of Labor.

1. Under the "I'm really not sure" section, choose START.
2. Be sure to read the directions as you proceed through the O*NET Interest Profiler.
3. Record your scores from the survey.

Realistic	Investigative	Artistic	Social	Enterprising	Conventional

Read about your two (2) highest scoring areas and record the characteristics of each area

Area #1 -	Area #2 -

Career Choices

As you proceed through the survey, use the chart to jot down pertinent information you discover about the careers you chose.

	Career Choice #1	Career Choice #2	Career Choice #3
Job Duties			
Knowledge			
Basic Skills			
Abilities			
Personality			
Educational Level			
Job Outlook			
Average Salary			

Module 4: College Planning

Colleges - Technical vs. Community College vs. University

"I think a college education is important no matter what you do in life."
Phil Mickelson

Now that you have a better idea of what careers you are interested in pursuing, you can begin researching colleges that offer your intended major. There are multiple paths to obtaining your certifications and/or degrees. Technical schools offer hands-on training in various trades. Some students pursue dual enrollment (enrolled in high school and college at the same time) while in high school and obtain specialized certifications before they graduate. For example, a student who is interested in becoming a doctor may enroll at a technical school and become a Certified Nursing Assistant. This will afford them the opportunity to work in their field of choice and gain valuable experience. Some technical schools offer specialized articulation agreements with colleges that allow you to transfer credits you have earned into your college program of study. If you make the right choices, the amount of time you actually spend in college could be lessened.

It is imperative that you know what each college requires for admission so that you can prepare accordingly. If you discover the college you are interested in attending requires you to have three years of a foreign language instead of two, you will be able to complete the extra year to meet the requirements. If you discover the minimum SAT math score is 840, you can measure your progress each time you take the SAT or you can sign up for an SAT prep class to help you better prepare to meet the score requirement.

College admission requirements vary from college to college and from state to state. Colleges receive many applications and the admissions process is very competitive. When you do your research, you become informed and put yourself in a position to do what it takes to be accepted to whatever college you plan to attend. Finding out important information such as GPA requirements at the last minute could limit your chances for admission. In addition to meeting the admissions requirements, some applications ask you to answer one or more essay questions. The writing skills you acquire in school will be very beneficial during this time. Follow the guidelines for answering discussion questions that we discussed in the test taking strategies section. This again is your time to show the application committee why you should be admitted to their college.

Be sure to schedule plenty of college visits so that you can actually spend time on the campus. You may have a different impression of the college once you have spent time there. Be sure to visit while students are still on campus so that you will get a true glimpse into what attending college there would be like. Choosing the right school or college is a big decision. Keep in mind you could possibly live there for four years of your life. Make every effort to be as educated as possible regarding what level of education you will need to land your dream career.

This college research activity will give you an introduction into performing college research. You should do this for every college you are interested in attending. You will be able to find this information by going to the colleges' website or by using various state funded college planning websites. Information is provided so that prospective students can make educated decisions regarding furthering their education.

How to Find Out More About a College

There are various ways of obtaining information about colleges. You can search for colleges in your state that offer the major you intend to pursue, go to your states college planning site, or go to the actual website of the college. Many college research websites place all the pertinent information in one location to make the research process much simpler.

	Technical School	**Community College**	**University**
Name of Institute			
Location of Institute			
Website			
Application Deadline and Fee			
Average SAT scores			
Average ACT scores			
In-state Tuition/Fees			
Out-of-State Tuition/Fees			
Room/Board Costs			
Other charges/fees			
Entrance difficulty			
Do they offer Financial Aid?			
Average Financial Aid amount awarded to Freshmen			

	Technical School	**Community College**	**University**
What High School courses do I need in order to meet the admissions requirements?			
Number of Undergraduate students			
Can I obtain my master's degree here also?			
What major(s) am I interested in pursuing?			

Module 4: College Planning

College Costs/Financial Aid/Scholarships

"I was President of the schools in junior high and high school, got a scholarship to New York University, played a little basketball, and was a celebrity.
Louis Gossett, Jr.

The next step in the college planning process is determine how to pay for college without going into debt. Many people are unaware of the many costs associated with attending college. Not only is there a tuition cost, but there are housing costs, costs associated with your meal plan, and various fees that must be paid before you can attend class. If you do not secure an adequate amount of grants and scholarships, you will be required to pay for the remaining balance out of pocket or through the use of government/private loans. You want to do everything possible to avoid having to take out loans. If you are willing to go the extra mile by applying the strategies you are learning and get involved in extra-curricular activities you will have a greater chance of attending college free of charge.

When you schedule your college visit, be sure to visit the Office of Admissions and Financial Aid. The counselors in these offices will be able to provide you with information regarding grants and scholarships that are available. They will also discuss important deadlines and special requirements that you should keep in mind such as completing the Free Application for Federal Student Aid (FAFSA). Students seeking financial aid should fill this application out as soon as possible. Make a commitment to get all of your information in well before the deadlines. Some of the grants are first come first served and once the funds are depleted, no other awards can be made.

There are many scholarship opportunities available. Some are based on financial need or athletic ability, while others are awarded based on merit. In order to be awarded a scholarship, you must meet the requirements. Requirements may range anywhere from the basics: high school GPA, extra-curricular activities, community service hours, and leadership roles held, to more specific requirements such as age, gender, college major, state, etc. Scholarship committees will be seeking students who performed well academically while sacrificing their free time to help strengthen their school and community. You may also speak with your high school counselor or visit your schools' college and career center for more information regarding local community scholarships that may be available. The more scholarship applications you submit the more likely you are to be selected as a scholarship recipient. Remember, once you are selected to receive a scholarship, you must continue to meet the requirements each year in order to continue receiving the financial assistance.

Just as the college application process is very competitive so is the scholarship selection process. Spend time visiting the financial aid portion of the colleges website, they will list the scholarships they offer for freshman students and the selection requirements. If you are knowledgeable of the requirements years before you actually apply, you will be able to take the necessary measures to meet the requirements. If the scholarship requires two or three years of verifiable community service, it will be impossible to meet that requirement if you find out about it your senior year.

In this scholarship research activity, you will need to access two college websites and navigate to their financial aid page. Look up two merit scholarships that are offered to freshman applicants and record your findings. In addition, research two local scholarships that are available in your community. Information on these scholarships may be listed on your local high school website counselors page.

Finding Scholarships

	College Scholarship #1	College Scholarship #2	Community Scholarship #1	Community Scholarship #2
Scholarship Name				
Award Amount				
Renewable Y/N				
Application Deadline				
HS GPA Requirement				
Number of Community Service Hours required				
Essay Question Topic(s)				
Other special requirements				

Module 4: College Planning

ACT and SAT Preparation

"The SAT is not perfect. We all know smart, knowledgeable people who do badly on standardized tests. But neither is it useless. SAT scores do measure both specific knowledge and valuable thinking skills." **Virginia Postrel**

Many colleges require you to take an entrance exam. These exams help colleges predict your readiness for college academics. Based on your scores, colleges can accept or deny your application. Some colleges may even require you to take and pass provisional courses before you can actually begin your college courses.

Many high schools offer ACT/SAT prep courses. They may be offered during the day or as an after school opportunity. Make an appointment with your counselor to discuss your options for taking a prep course. If you do not have access to a course at your school, there are various online prep courses that can help you prepare for the exam. Understanding how to take the exams is a key component to obtaining a good score. Many tools and resources are available on the ACT and SAT websites. Visit www.act.org for ACT test prep, registration and scores and visit www.collegeboard.com for test prep and information on taking the SAT. To register for the exams, you will need to create a profile on each of the sites. There is a testing fee for each exam and some assistance may be available to students who receive free or reduced meals.

Be sure to register and take the exams well before your senior year of high school. You do not want the only thing blocking your acceptance to the college or your choice or receiving a scholarship to be your inability to obtain the required exam score.

ACT/SAT Information

Go to each site to find the information you will need to complete the chart.

	ACT	SAT
Test Date		
Registration Deadline		
Cost		
Late Registration Deadline		
Late Registration Fee		

Module 5: Career Planning

Choosing the Right Career

"I did my first apprenticeship when I was 15, then joined the union when I was 17. I worked every summer in high school and college." **Christopher Reeve**

You have completed your interest inventory and have received valuable information that can be used as a guide to possible careers that fit your interests. How do you know if you will enjoy working in those careers? If you are interested in being a lawyer, seek a summer internship at a local law firm. You may be in the mailroom or filing documents all day; but, you will also be around people who are where you want to be in the future. You will be able to see them in action and gain a deeper understanding of the duties and demands of the career. Experience should be gained during your high school summers and while in college through summer jobs, internships, and apprenticeship programs.

Now is the time to begin outlining your strategy for getting the position you want. Some students do everything they are supposed to do and end up graduating from college unable to gain employment in their chosen field because they do not have any work experience pertinent to that career. Most college graduate entry level job descriptions call for applicants to have at least 6 months of experience. You're probably wondering how you can get experience if this is your first opportunity to enter into this field.

An internship is an opportunity to work at a company while you are still in high school or your undergraduate studies. Many internships are not paid; however, you will gain much needed experience which can prove to be more valuable than money when you graduate from college. An apprenticeship is generally a paid position that allows an apprentice to get hands-on experience working under the leadership and instruction of a professional who is deemed a master at his/her occupation. Internships and apprenticeships can last for periods of time ranging from six months to a year and upon successful completion may lead to a permanent position.

While on your college tours, take time to visit the colleges career center. There you will find information regarding employment opportunities on and off campus. Personnel specialized in resume writing, interviewing skills, and career search are available to help students transition successfully from college to the work force. They also have access to information regarding the internships, externships, and apprenticeship programs that are available. When you are given the opportunity to complete an internship with a company, you have the ability to show off your talents and expertise. You are able to network and meet people who can become references and speak on your behalf when you apply for permanent positions.

Some students have aspirations of joining the military and they plan on staying in until they retire. Many military personnel obtain their college degrees while serving their country. If you are interested in a career in the military, first determine if there is a JROTC program at your school. This will give you an introduction to the military and upon completion of the program, you could earn scholarships that help you pay for college. Many students are unaware of the opportunities that are available to men and women who join the armed forces. For every position in the civilian job market, there is probably an equivalent position in the military.

If you are interested in joining one of the branches of the military: Army, Navy, Air Force, Marine Corps, Coast Guard, or National Guard, contact a local recruiting officer. They can speak with you regarding your aspirations and help guide you in the right direction. Before you make the call, be sure to do your own research so you will be able to understand the information the recruiter is discussing. You can also share the information you discover with your parents. Be sure to speak with your school counselor about signing up and taking the Armed Services Vocational Aptitude Battery (ASVAB) test. This test measures your mental aptitude and gives the military an assessment of your skills and abilities. Your scores will determine which military careers best suit your skillset.

Reflection:
Based on your career choices, what types of internships will you set up for this summer? What companies will you contact?

_____
_____
_____
_____

Implementation:
Explore two branches of the military. Find two careers that you would be interested in pursuing. List the branches and careers you chose.

_____
_____
_____
_____

Culminating Assessment

Vision Board Project

"Visualize this thing that you want, see it, feel it, believe in it. Make your mental blueprint, and begin to build." **Robert Collier**

In this last module, you will create a visual representation of the things you would like to experience, obtain, and become. Use the information you discovered about soft skills, academic enrichment, goal setting, and your college and career choices to make your vision board become the blueprint you will follow on your journey to changing your desires into reality.

Your vision board will serve as a motivational roadmap that will inspire you to work hard at achieving the goals you have set for yourself. If you have aspirations of becoming a Pediatrician, each time you see the picture of the doctor with the babies, you will be able to envision yourself in that scene doing what you love to do. Each time you see the picture of students on the campus of the college you plan to attend, you will be able to picture yourself on campus accomplishing the goals you have set for yourself.

Vision boards serve as powerful tools because they keep your attention focused on what you want to manifest in your life. Your vision board should be placed in a location where you will see it multiple times each day and it should be saved on your electronic device. Each time you feel the pressure to quit, look at your vision board and find something that inspires you to keep pushing.

Materials Needed:
- 22x28 sized poster board or larger
- Magazines, Newspapers, Computer printouts, etc.
- Tape, Glue, Glitter, Scissors, Markers, construction and/or colored paper, etc.
- Anything other items that will inspire you to reach for your goals

Instructions:
1. Put together a list of images you would like to include on your vision board. Images from the following areas should be represented on your board.
   - Emotions/Quotes/Emoticons – these will represent how you want to feel
   - Interests – pictures/objects that represent your hobbies and interests
   - Colleges - photos/objects that represent the colleges you have selected
   - Careers – photos/objects that represent the careers you have selected
   - Lifestyle - photos/objects that represent where you want to live, your house, car, family, vacation choices, etc.
2. Use a blank sheet of paper to design the layout of your vision board

3. Select a minimum of 25 images that best illustrate the goals and dreams you have set for yourself.
4. Create text to describe your interests, lifestyle, colleges, careers, thoughts and feelings.
5. Arrange the images and words on the poster in a way that will be inspiring to you.

Final Reflection

"Without reflection, we go blindly on our way, creating more unintended consequences, and failing to achieve anything useful."
Margaret J. Wheatley

Write the future you a letter. Take a moment to reflect on all you have discovered about yourself through participation in the Start Right..Stay Right program. Discuss what you have learned throughout this process and how you plan to implement the tools and strategies into your life so that you can enjoy a bright future.

Closing Thoughts…..

Congratulations on completing the Start Right..Stay Right program!!!!

You are now equipped with best practices and highly effective tools that will empower you to gain more control over the outcomes you create for yourself. The lessons and activities you completed worked together to foster a solid foundation which will support your journey towards accomplishment of the goals and dreams you have set for yourself. Hold fast to the vision you have created for your life and remember…

"Failed plans should not be interpreted as a failed vision. Visions don't change, they are only refined. Plans rarely stay the same, and are scrapped or adjusted as needed. Be stubborn about the vision, but flexible with your plan."
John C. Maxwell

GLOSSARY
Cambridge Dictionary - http://dictionary.cambridge.org/us/

Module 1: Soft Skills
- **Integrity** - the quality of being honest and having strong moral principles
- **Honest** – (of a person) truthful or able to be trusted; not likely to steal, cheat, or lie, or (of actions, speech, or appearance) showing these qualities
- **Morals** – standards for good or bad character and behavior
- **Values** – the principles that help you to decide what is right and wrong, and how to act in various situations
- **Conflict** – an active disagreement, as between opposing opinions or needs
- **Resolution** – the act of solving a problem or finding a way to improve a difficult situation
- **Communicate** – to give messages or information to others through speech, writing, body movements, or signals
- **Critical thinking** – the process of thinking carefully about a subject or idea, without allowing feelings or opinions to affect you
- **Problem solving** – the process of finding solutions to problems
- **Predict** – to say that an event or action will happen in the future
- **Inference** – a belief or opinion that you develop from the information that you know
- **Decision** – something you choose; a choice
- **Consequence** – a result of an action or situation
- **Teamwork** – the combined actions of a group of people working together effectively to achieve a goal
- **Work ethic** - the belief that work is valuable as an activity and is morally good
- **Time Management** – the practice of using the time that you have available in a useful and effective way, especially in your work
- **Prioritize** – to arrange in order of importance so that you can deal with the most important things before the others

Module 2: Academic Enrichment
- **Reading** – the skill or activity of getting information from written words
- **Annotate** – to add notes or remarks on a piece of writing
- **Comprehend** – to understand something completely
- **Retention** – the ability to keep or continue having something
- **Relevance** – the degree to which something is related or useful to what is happening or being talked about
- **Retention** – the ability to keep or continue having something
- **Study** – to learn a particular subject or subjects, esp. in a school or college or by reading books

- **Grade Point Average (GPA)** – a number giving the average quality of a student's work, used to calculate rank in class
- **Test** – a set of questions or practical activities that show what someone knows or what someone or something can do
- **Anxiety** – an uncomfortable feeling of worry about something that is happening or might happen
- **Cram** – to try to learn a lot very quickly before an exam
- **Tutorial** – a period of study with a tutor involving one student or a small group
- **Enrich** – to improve the quality of something by adding something else
- **Resource** – something that can be used to help you

Module 3: Goal Setting
- **Goal** – an aim or purpose
- **Goal Setting** – the process of deciding what you want to achieve or what you want someone else to achieve over a particular period
- **Resolution** – the act of solving a problem or finding a way to improve a difficult situation
- **Accountable** – responsible for and having to explain your actions
- **Short-term** – happening, existing, or continuing for only a little time
- **Long-term** – happening, existing, or continuing for many years or far into the future
- **Motivate** – willingness to do something, or something that causes such willingness
- **Intrinsic** – basic to a thing, being an important part of making it what it is
- **Extrinsic** – coming from outside, or not related to something
- **Academics** – the subjects that you study in high school or college

Module 4: College Planning
- **Interests** – a feeling of having your attention held by something, or of wanting to be involved with and learn more about something
- **Survey** – a set of questions people are asked to gather information or find out their opinions, or the information gathered by asking many people the same questions
- **Job** – the regular work that a person does to earn money
- **Career** – a job for which you are trained and in which it is possible to advance during your working life, so that you get greater responsibility and earn more money
- **Technical school** – a school where students learn skills that involve working with their hands
- **Community college** – a local two-year college at which students can learn a skill or prepare to enter a university

- **University** – a place of higher education usually for people who have finished twelve years of schooling and where they can obtain more knowledge and skills, and get a degree to recognize this
- **Tuition** – the money paid for being taught, especially at a college or university
- **Fee** – an amount of money charged for a service of for the use of something
- **Room and Board** – a charge for renting a room and the cost of meals
- **Financial Aid** – official help given to a person, organization, or country in the form of money, loans, reduced taxes, etc.
- **Scholarship** – money given to someone to help pay for that person's education
- **Grant** – a sum of money given by the government, a university, or a private organization to another organization or person for a special purpose
- **Loan** – an act of lending something, esp. a sum of money that has to be paid back with interest
- **Interest** – an additional amount of money that is a percentage of the amount borrowed
- **Advanced Placement (AP) courses** – a program for students offering courses that are equal to college courses
- **Entrance exam** – an exam that you take to be accepted into a school, etc.
- **ACT** – www.act.org
- **SAT** – www.collegeboard.com

Module 5: Career Planning
- **Internship** – a period of time spent receiving or completing training at a job as a part of becoming qualified to do it
- **Apprentice** – someone works for an expert to learn a particular skill or job

Culminating Assessment: Vision Board Project
- **Vision** – an imagined mental image of something
- **Representation** – a sign, picture, model, etc. of something
- **Storyboard** – a series of drawings of images showing the planned order of images
- **Illustrate** – to show the meaning or truth of something more clearly by giving examples

Final Reflection
- **Reflection** – careful thoughts

www.ingramcontent.com/pod-product-compliance
Lightning Source LLC
Chambersburg PA
CBHW080351170426
43194CB00014B/2749